DRAGON SLAYING
A BETTER WAY TO MANAGE

A MANAGEMENT MODEL TO SYSTEMATICALLY
IMPROVE PERFORMANCE AND PROFITS

Do you have a practical theory of management by which to lead your organisation?

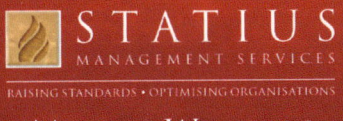

STATIUS
MANAGEMENT SERVICES
RAISING STANDARDS • OPTIMISING ORGANISATIONS

MARK WOODS

Order this book online at www.trafford.com
or email orders@trafford.com

Most Trafford titles are also available at major online book retailers.

© Copyright 2011 Mark Woods

All rights reserved. No part of this publication may be reproduced, stored in a retrieval system, or transmitted, in any form or by any means, electronic, mechanical, photocopying, recording, or otherwise, without the written prior permission of the author.

Printed in the United States of America.

ISBN: 978-1-4269-5905-9

Library of Congress Control Number: 2011903752

Trafford rev. 07/15/2011

 www.trafford.com

North America & international
toll-free: 1 888 232 4444 (USA & Canada)
phone: 250 383 6864 ♦ fax: 812 355 4082

Dragon Slaying
A better way to manage:
A management model to systematically improve performance and profits

Do you have a *practical* theory of management by which to lead your organisation?

Contents

Foreword vi
Preface viii
Acknowledgements. xi
Introduction and aims of this book 1
The benefits of applying this model 1

Part One: Scene setting: challenging management thinking 3
    The challenge. 3
    The management model for driving performance improvement 4

Part Two: Understanding the organisation as a system 9
    The organisational purpose 12

Part Three: Understanding people 15

Part Four: Understanding variation. 21
    Cause and effect 22
    Two types of variation 27
    Targets, specifications, the voice of the customer and the voice of the process . . . 29

Part Five: Understanding learning 33
    From chaos to order and prediction 35

Part Six: Dragon slaying 39
    Management myths 40
    Conclusion 43

References. 44

List of figures and illustrations

Fig. 1   The four components of the management model
Fig. 2   The four components inextricably linked
Fig. 3   The four components fused together revealing the organisation's purpose
Fig. 4   The systems diagram
Fig. 5   Maslow's Hierarchy of Needs
Fig. 6   Cause-Effect – oversimplified
Fig. 7   Cause-Effect and the effect of time
Fig. 8   The Cause-Effect or Fishbone Diagram
Fig. 9   A Cause-Effect diagram showing the potential causes of performance variation in a call centre
Fig.10   The process prediction chart™
Fig.11   The Plan, Do, Study, Act (PDSA) model for learning
Fig.12   From chaos to order and prediction
Fig.13   The Performance Dashboard®
Fig.14   Connected measurement systems: How different levels of management need different perspectives and add value differently

For my long suffering wife, Nicky, a Deming widow,
for Stinkbomb, Monkey Dog and the Tiggster.

For Brian Wood
(I hope I have done you justice)

Foreword

The first recession of the 21st century has been quite different to any of those in the second half of the 20th century and the recovery needs to be different too. The balance between the state, business and society needs to shift to a completely new equilibrium where business accepts a bigger role in shaping our future.

Currently, too many businesses have structures and management styles that:

- Encourage different internal functions to compete with each other to secure finance, resources and strategic influence

- Unintentionally stifle individual entrepreneurship and fail to provide a strong value set with which their people can identify

- Create reactive rather than proactive behaviours managing through metrics that are more about past shortcomings than future opportunities

- Protect the status quo rather than encouraging a dynamic learning culture that anticipates new possibilities for growth and change. Yet organisations cannot stand still; they either prosper or shrink, which is why so few see their 50th birthday!

One reason for this, stemming from traditional educational thinking in schools and colleges, is that managers make a merit of analytical approaches to decision making. They dissect a business issue looking at all the component parts – financial return, resources required, risk profile, etc – with 'go/no go' thresholds for each. Managers address each according to their own disciplines, accountancy, marketing, HR or operations. This approach may accumulate a lot of knowledge or data but it often contributes little to understanding.

Understanding an organisation and which opportunities it should seize and which it should reject needs a more holistic approach that recognises that the organisation is an organic thing, living within an organic environment. Understanding how people and teams interact to achieve goals – or miss them - requires a more appropriate management technique. And we need successful, self aware organisations to play that new role in our future that I referred to at the outset.

Mark's book is a very readable and pragmatic introduction to the world of 'systems thinking' as it applies to organisations.

It will greatly assist young managers keen to succeed. It will also encourage those who, like me, are older and 'wiser' to reappraise whether we have become blind to the limitations of the passably successful management model that we have applied in our careers to date. It is refreshing that Mark is not presenting himself as a management guru, though he has respect for some who have earned that title, but as an enlightened practitioner. He presents real world examples and is anxious to discuss his ideas with anyone who would like to do so. He tells me that the second edition of the book is already on the drawing board with numerous fresh, in depth, case studies. He hopes that some of you will get in touch and bring views and practical experience that merit being shared in the next publication.

So, don't just be a passive reader, engage with Mark and become part of the story!

Keith Faulkner CBE FRSA

Preface

Ever since I can remember, I have been fascinated by building things and understanding how things work. My father was a Chief Engineer in the merchant navy and, during holidays, we were forever making forays into foreign fields and, on the ship, between ports, I would be sat on the floor, ship rolling, and I'd be making something from Lego. From Lego I graduated to Meccano (although always preferred Lego), from Meccano to woodwork, from woodwork to metalwork. As an apprentice engineer, also in the merchant navy, I was interested by and trained in the workings of main engines, diesel generators, gearboxes, heating and refrigeration systems - anything and everything necessary to run a ship and keep it afloat.

Sadly, however, my career in the navy coincided with the demise of the British shipping fleet and the 1980's recession. I then took a degree in mechanical and production engineering where I became enthralled with the (still unexploited) potential of castable and machineable ceramics. On completion of my studies, I took a job as an 'agent of change' in a factory that had seen pretty much no change since the War. The brief was to make the diamond tooling being produced faster, cheaper and better quality. As with many engineers, on my journey from Lego to tooling, I had been focused on the technology and on the task; for me, it was all about getting the job done.

Needless to say, as I moved into the world of teams and later management, I began to realise that, in order to get the job done, you need to take the people with you. As a result, I became more curious about management styles, people and how they tick. I then took an MBA at Bradford to cement my understanding of management and develop my people skills. It didn't do much for the people skills, that came later with an ongoing interest in Neuro Linguistic Programming (NLP), but it certainly gave me a much wider appreciation of the art of management.

I walked out of the MBA into another recession of the early '90s. After four hundred job applications, I decided to set up as a freelance consultant on the back of the UK's DTI Enterprise Initiative selling my services to organisations wishing to develop quality management systems.

I had been working in the field of management systems for a number of years with (even if I say so myself) a certain degree of success and, a few years ago, I was looking to take my company, Statius Management Services, to the next level. A chance encounter with Norman Speirs led to my re-acquaintance with the teachings of Deming and a passion for both Deming and systems thinking was reawakened.

As I began to read and reread books, papers and articles by Deming, Henry Neave, Don Wheeler, Brian Joiner, Alfie Kohn, Denis Sherwood, John Seddon and many others, as well as much of the back catalogue of the British Deming

Association and latterly the Deming Forum, I was drawn deeper into the Deming community. I found myself awed and excited (my wife would probably say transfixed) by the prospect of the practical application of Deming and systems thinking to the development of the business.

At the same time, my company had reached a milestone at which point I knew I would start looking for a chairman to mentor me in order to take the company to this, in my mind, elusive next level.

I then attended a seminar on performance management at the then Institute of Quality Assurance (IQA) (now the Chartered Institute of Quality (CQI)) presented by Brian Wood. I approached Brian and arranged to have lunch with him to see if he knew anyone that could mentor me. At the lunch I made my case to Brian and it very quickly became apparent that he did not know anyone suitable, at which point, because I knew I would be paying for lunch, I was somewhat deflated. Brian had other ideas. Brian was on the verge of retiring and offered to teach me all he knew... for free. Very quickly the penny dropped and we could both see how we could marry our skill sets of management systems and performance management to deliver even greater value to clients.

The seed of what would become a core Statius service, Optimisation 3D™, had been germinated. For the next few years, we worked in developing both the existing Statius team, and an additional associate team, around the Deming philosophy and systems thinking.

At this point it should be said that to some Deming is taken as Gospel. I'd certainly not put myself in that camp; we are not wedded to everything Deming said and, since his passing, the world has moved on; globalisation, changes to the social contract between individuals and organisations, the internet, social networking, mobile phones, PDA's are just a few post Deming developments. Indeed, where we challenge the Deming view or find that it needs a modern context, we have commissioned independent studies, most notably from Kingston University, to update our thinking.

For me, the bottom line is that Deming is one of the few management thinkers to provide a holistic and fully inclusive theory of management with which to lead an organisation. Additionally, any philosophy of management that has at its heart the presuppositions of "joy in work" and "joy in learning" must be essentially liberating of the creativity and talent so often suppressed.

I now find myself at a point where, with prospects, clients, suppliers and consultants, I have considerably more useful, and considerably more insightful, conversations about the way in which organisations are managed; about how work works.

However, because of the sometimes counter intuitive nature of Deming's thinking, I was driven by my own personal requirement to distil down what (little) I know (despite being a voracious reader) into a short, simple and, hopefully, lucid and useful exploration of the ideas we now employ about how to manage an organisation. Inevitably, as I began to jot down my thoughts, the ideas evolved and the project became ever larger. This book is the result.

Additionally, in order to get time pressed senior executives to think about how the work works in their organisations, the Optimisation team have invented and published the Coffee Break Challenge. This is a series of questions that you might ask yourself about your organisation. It is available on our website (www.statius.uk.com) with no registration or fee. The challenge is simply designed to make you think about your organisation.

Please be the judge on whether or not I have succeeded AND, please, let me have your thoughts, I can be contacted on 0044 7976 426 286 or mwoods@statius.uk.com.

Take the Coffee Break Challenge at www.statius.uk.com

Acknowledgements

As ever, there are many people who need thanking and the danger is leaving someone out! If I have done so, it is entirely due to my failing memory and nothing to do with their (your) valued contribution.

Without doubt, this book would not have been written without the chance meeting of the late Brian Wood, a mentor, father figure, perfectionist and inspiration. A tragic and untimely loss. I miss you.

Obviously, the journey to publication has not been without challenge or revision. Initial drafts were circulated to a number of trusted colleagues for review and feedback. All have helped me develop greater insight and add clarity to my understanding of some of the, often counter intuitive, aspects of Deming's thinking and these include Dr Peter Worthington, Stuart Swalwell and Prof David Kerridge. Thank you all for your help and guidance.

Dr Peter Worthington and the team at PRISM Europe Consultancy also need thanking for the use of their WinChart® and Performance Dashboard® software and the accompanying screenshots used in the text. Peter also needs thanking for elevating the term Dragon Slaying, buried deep in the text, to the book's title - inspirational.

The irritatingly creative Simon Shimmens needs thanking not just for the brilliant idea of getting kids to draw pictures of dragons as chapter markers, but also for getting Keith Faulkner on board to write the considered and insightful foreword. Thanks Keith.

Thanks, too, to the team at Kingston University: the lovely Charlene Edwards for her enduring help and assistance and for putting myself and Brian in touch with Prof Katie Truss and our brilliant, diligent researcher Amanda Rosewarne.

I would also like to thank my long-suffering office manager, Cathy Proto, for her eagle eye and consummate understanding and her valiant efforts to improve my understanding of English, spelling and the rules of grammar.

The guys (and girls) at Red and Green Marketing for their sterling work on the Coffee Break Challenge and the pictures and images contained herein.

Thanks too to Pamela Quick of the MIT Press Permissions department for authorising the Optimisation Team to use and reference the works of Dr Deming.

Penultimately, big big thanks to the publishing team at Trafford without whom this would not have been possible.

Finally, thanks to Nicky, my wife, and to my children for their patience and understanding.

Introduction and aims of this book

It may be disingenuous, but many managers, however they get into the position, just get on with the job of "managing"; there is often little underlying structure or thought given to how or what or who to manage. As so eloquently argued in an email from Prof David Kerridge:

> "Existing management skills are often based on being good in a crisis; it is more important to be swift and decisive than to be right. It is much better to learn how to prevent the crises happening, but, as one manager (who did make the transition successfully) told me "it is really disorientating".

The aim of this book is to improve our approach to management:

- By suggesting a framework for managing organisations
- By developing the framework into a holistic and integrated management model that can be applied in order to engage staff, create a learning environment and, ultimately, drive improvements in performance

The benefits of applying this model

There are a number of potential benefits following the application of this model:

- A more informed understanding of how an organisation delivers value to customers and stakeholders; how the work in an organisation works
- The development of a strategy for "Listening to Customers and Stakeholders"
- The development of the organisation in which everyone's efforts result in:
    - Improved performance
    - Less stress
    - Improved profit

Improved profits result from a more engaged workforce focused on the purpose of the organisation, constantly striving to deliver better performance and *knowing* that they have, or have not, done so.

Drawing by Miss Frankie Meek, age 10

Part One
Scene setting: challenging management thinking

"Imagine that it is now the year 1870. Pasteur has only recently demonstrated that fermentation is caused by organisms which are carried in the air. Only a few months ago, Lister tried out the first antiseptic, carbolic acid, and found that it worked to prevent inflammation and pus after surgery.

The spread of medical information was much slower 120 years ago than it is today. Imagine you are a young researcher in medical school in the USA. The civil war has just finished and you are trying to develop your own career after army service. You are a serious young doctor who tried to learn the latest developments in your profession. Suppose that you have just learnt about Pasteur's and Lister's work and that you have been invited to speak to a group of distinguished physicians, many of them having become famous for their heroic service as surgeons during the Civil War. What you now understand from your studies is that these famous physicians are actually killing their patients. Your responsibility is to explain to them, if you can, that, because they do not wash their hands or sterilise their instruments, they sew death into every wound. Your assignment is to persuade them to forget most of what they have been taught, to abandon much of the wisdom they have accumulated over their distinguished careers and rebuild their understanding of the practice of medicine around the new theory of germs." [1]

The challenge

Hopefully, without being too dramatic, this is the position I find myself in. I am the (not so) young doctor and you are the eminent physicians.

Let me lay my cards on the table. If you are willing to indulge me for the short time it takes to read this book, I am pretty sure I will challenge your current thinking (unless, of course, you are already familiar with the work of Dr W. Edwards Deming). I am pretty sure you will ask some difficult questions which I may struggle to answer; and I am absolutely sure even, if you do agree with me, it will not be easy or quick to improve your organisations.

If you are looking for quick and easy fixes to your management problems, please read no further.

In a short introduction to Deming and systems thinking, I may not totally convince you of the 'truth' of my argument but I do hope to challenge your world view and stimulate your desire to learn more. If I am really lucky, I may even change your whole approach to managing yourself ……and your organisation!

The management model for driving performance improvement

Enhancing the performance of any organisation requires a structured and systematic approach. However,

> *"Efforts and methods of improvement of quality and productivity are in most companies and in most government agencies fragmented, with no overall competent guidance, no integrated system for continual improvement ... people go off in different directions, unaware of what other people are doing". [2]*

In essence, the conceptual framework of management is impoverished. Fundamentally, it is difficult to connect what each of us do on a day-to-day level with

a) our efforts to improve the way in which we undertake work and
b) our efforts to satisfy customers.

Fortunately, there is an antidote. It is based on both the need to understand the 'trade-offs' necessary to attain optimum performance and on four fundamental principles, arguably irrefutable laws, of management:

- Understanding an organisation as a network of connected parts
- Understanding people and why they behave as they do
- Understanding variation; a *real* understanding of the key performance indicators and their predictive abilities
- Understanding how an organisation learns and improves

These four principles are inextricably interlinked and, as in any system, the strength of the whole rests not in the strength of the individual principles but in the strength of the relationships and the interactions between them.

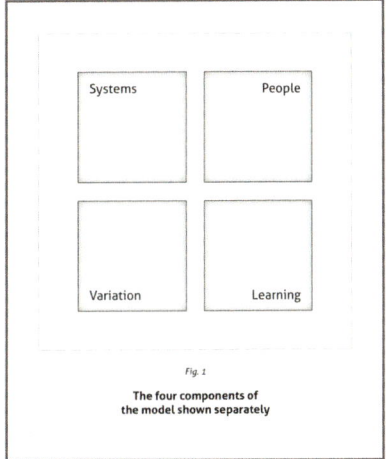
Fig. 1
The four components of the model shown separately

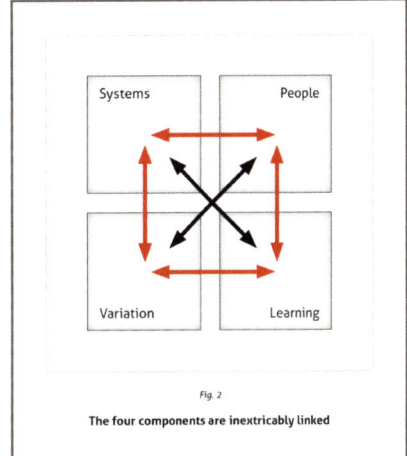
Fig. 2
The four components are inextricably linked

Figure 1 shows the four components. Figure 2 shows how each component of the model is connected to all other parts; an idea that is explored throughout the text. Figure 3 fuses the four components to reveal the centre-piece, the overlap, the organisational glue, which binds the four components together. This organisational glue is the organisation's purpose or aim.

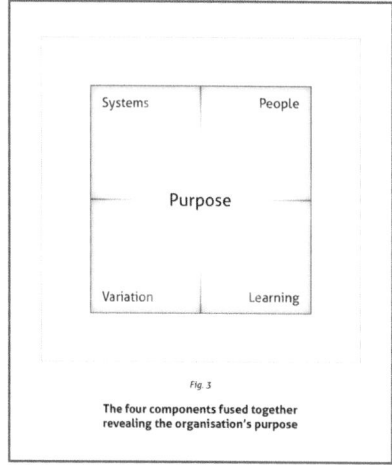

Fig. 3
The four components fused together revealing the organisation's purpose

Many people new to this thinking sometimes conclude, initially, that this is no more than just 'common sense'. (To quote Dr Deming "If it's common sense then why isn't everyone doing it"? – London 1986.) However, managing in accordance with these principles is, in our experience, very rare. The mantra of the day (the approach and behaviours) of the average manager is driven by aggressive competition and short-term thinking and, in reality, most of what drives the current mantra makes sense, both in isolation and until people stop to think about it.

I hope to show the folly of the current mantra and that knowledge of any one of the above principles is incomplete without knowledge of the others - you need to appreciate the whole.

Drawing by Megan Harman, age 6

Part Two
Understanding the organisation as a system

The traditional "picture" of an organisation is the organisation chart or family tree. The first recorded use of such a chart was after a train crash in Massachusetts in 1841 [3]. An investigation was headed by a Major Whistler in order to establish the causes of the accident. Major Whistler designed an organisation chart to describe functional responsibility with the sole purpose of apportioning blame should another incident occur. To this day, the focus of the organisation chart remains control; that is, to ensure people do their jobs and do them properly. 150 plus years later and we are still employing the same thinking!

Additionally, as was recently noted by John Seddon, "if we design work into functions and give each function its own target, should we be surprised if they don't co-operate with one another". [4]

That's not to say that the organisation chart is without merit but research has suggested there is a better diagram which supports a more enlightened approach delivering a more sustained performance.

In contrast to the family tree, a systems diagram shows the flow of relationships ***through*** the organisation and highlights the need for internal departments to treat one another as suppliers and customers. The systems diagram shows the interactions that are needed to optimise the organisational system: if the internal suppliers can understand their internal customer needs, real step changes can be made. Organisations are not optimised when each department is looking after its own self interest. Any attempt to isolate and analyse components of an organisation, as suggested by the traditional family tree, is ineffective. In a post-race analysis, Lewis Hamilton will critically review all aspects of the race. Team Hamilton's objective is to ensure the "system" works to achieve the aim, that is to win the race. This necessitates recognising that, to optimise the whole system, the pre-race planning, the set up of the car, the driver, the pit crew, the trainers and the support crew need to work together in harmony. These individual components of the system cannot all be delivering at 100% all of the time.

Similarly, it would be sacrilege to remove the timpani section of the London Philharmonic from the 1812 overture, Bono the singer from the rock band U2, or the fielder at silly mid-off simply because they are not delivering *all* of the time. In these instances, there is a recognition (that is sometimes lacking in management) that individual components of the system may need to be sub optimised (sometimes, just temporarily) in order to ensure that the whole system is optimised.
If an organisation (and that means everyone within the organisation!) is to truly learn, it will need to ensure policies, procedures and measurement systems support the optimisation of the entire system, not of particular departments or divisions.

This thinking of the organisation as a system, and the systems diagram in particular (Fig. 4), maps the critical value adding processes that the organisation needs to undertake in order to satisfy its customers. These critical processes can then be linked to the performance measurement system and associated operational or ISO type procedures. The beauty of the systems diagram is that it becomes a window into the organisation showing the sequence of events required to deliver value to the client, customer or stakeholder; it shows the feedback loops inherent in an organisation and, critically, it shows how the work works.

It may be that some processes, particularly the core value adding processes, will be made up of or include a number of subprocesses, each of which may be flowcharted to detail inputs, outputs and any lower level feedback loops. This enables the hierarchy of processes to be mapped. This is important because the strength of the system comes from its interconnections - its relationships. Each process is a sequence or chain of operations needed to produce a particular outcome, for example, taking an order, delivering a service, making a component or preparing an invoice. Costs, waste and profit are all outputs from these processes but, instead of placing the emphasis of effort on the output, the emphasis should be on ensuring everyone is focused on understanding the customers' needs and improving how the work gets done: working on the way work works. Essentially, management needs to manage not just departments and functions, but also, and critically, the interconnections between them. Consequently, and this is critical, each component in the process should be judged on the basis of its contribution to the whole system, not on its performance considered in isolation.

The best example of a system that works to perfection is the human body. It always works to balance itself against any intrusion that would jeopardise its existence. Not one organ is more important than the others, yet some systems can have certain non-essential organs removed and still remain functionally successful, e.g. one kidney, a gall bladder, partial liver, etc. There are organs that, when removed from the system, stop the system from functioning - heart, brain, lungs. These organs of the system are the foundation from which all other organs receive instructions. They balance input versus output, regulate and manipulate consumables and waste, and "call to arms" all energy and functions of the system to do battle where it is needed the most at any given time (infections, poisons, perforations, etc). The body is a perfect example of teamwork! [5]

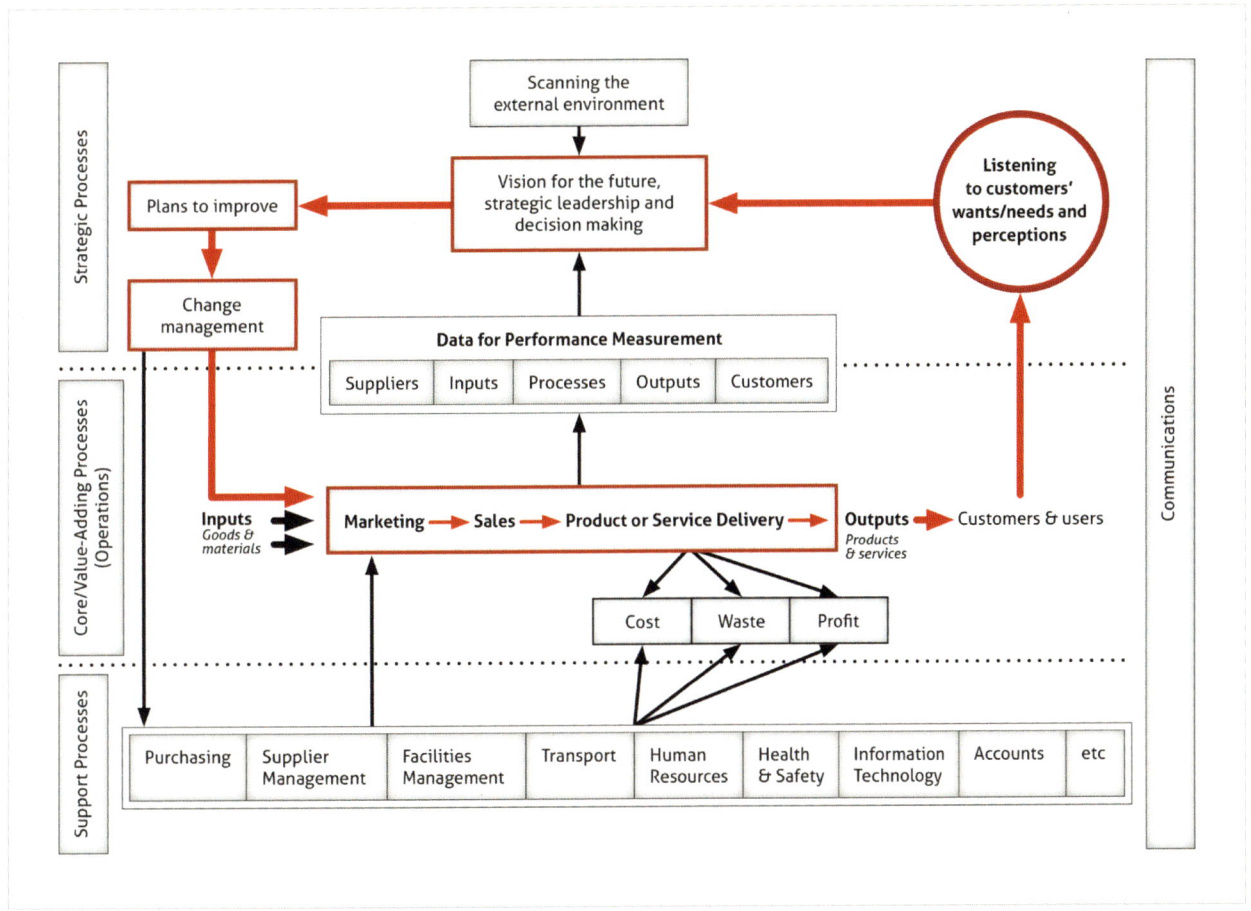

Fig. 4

The Systems Diagram

The systems diagram has been adapted from diagrams in W. Edwards Deming's Out of the Crisis and Alan Clark's Picture Your Business.

Incidentally, returning to the systems diagram, we encourage organisations to place it on their desktops and then run both their procedures and measurement dashboards from there using the Performance Dashboard®.

The benefit of the systems diagram is that it eliminates any departmental silo thinking replacing it with interdepartmental teamwork. Efforts to optimise the organisation are then focused on the system which, in turn, focuses on the customer in accordance with the organisation's purpose or aim.

In its simplest form "think in systems, work on processes".

The organisational purpose

We often find that leaders, managers and directors will intuitively say that the purpose or aim of the system is to make a profit. But anyone can make a profit - slash costs. Slashing costs will deliver short-term profit but at long term expense. The optimisation of an organisation requires a balanced approach to short, medium and long-term goals.

In adopting the traditional profit centred approach, objectives are typically set by top managers and broken down through a chain of command which makes managers and individual workers accountable for the achievement of accounting based targets. The whole emphasis is on hierarchy and control with departments and divisions attempting to carry out the, often conflicting, objectives of senior managers.

Our view of an organisation is different. An organisation is:

- People working together within systems and processes in order to accomplish a purpose or an aim

Therefore, the traditional hierarchical, departmental functional approach is turned on its head to support this living and organic organisation.

What we are looking to establish is: What are the *benefits or capabilities* that your customers get from the products or services you provide? Essentially, we need the organisation's PURPOSE defined from the customer's point of view.

A number of examples follow:

- A lift company's purpose might be:
  - Transporting people and goods in buildings and structures, effortlessly
- Rolls-Royce or Bentley might consider their purpose to be:
  - The ability to travel in luxury in your own vehicle
- An architect's purpose might be:
  - Providing better places in which to live, work, shop, learn or in which to just to meet one another
    - Another architectural practice may consider their aim to be
  - Prestigious, innovative buildings in which to work
    - Yet another practice might think their purpose to be
  - Leading edge, sustainable building solutions

The purpose or aim is critically important as it determines the organisation's boundary and its processes. The reasons for including three different aims for architects is to show that organisations undertaking similar work may have dramatically different aims which directly impact on the processes employed.

Like, but different to, an organisation's mission or vision statement, the purpose or aim of the organisation should motivate and direct people in the organisation in pursuit of a common goal. It has been suggested [6] that the questions required to "test" a purpose are:

- Does the purpose reflect customer wants and desires?
- Is what the purpose suggests worth doing?
- Does the purpose reach for the hearts and minds of people who work for the organisation?
- Is the purpose noble and does it serve the public?

Very few companies develop aims which meet these criteria so, by default, they don't have a purpose which aligns the effort of people to the organisation. As a result, very few companies achieve their full potential. If you don't have an intended destination, any road will take you there.

name Fred

Drawing by Tom Mackenzie, age 7

Part Three
Understanding people

How many times do you hear organisations say that "*People are our most precious resource*"?

How many times do you really believe it?

Undoubtedly, people ***should*** be the most precious resource, along with time: people, because they are the only source of creativity, innovation and improvement, and time, because it cannot be stored, i.e. each moment is a one off which will never recur.

So how do we manage people? As already noted above, traditional management tends to be "controlling". The belief system, and consequently motivation, starts with the thinking "how can we make the workforce follow our instructions and our orders"?

We would suggest a different starting point and a different belief system:

- People work best when the system has been designed *with them* to help them execute their tasks more easily
- We are all different (thankfully): we have different experiences and values (all of which are valuable); we learn differently and we go about our work in different ways
- An organisation can only learn if its people learn
- If you need instructions, procedures and/or standing orders detailing how the work works, it is best to involve staff in their creation

If we want to truly understand people and for them to help us improve the system, we need, above anything else, to understand how they learn. There are only five ways into the brain and each is through one of the five senses. In management, however, we tend not to smell or taste our way to success. The three dominant senses for learning are therefore:

- Through verbal explanations – auditory
- Through demonstration or active involvement – kinaesthetic
- Through graphic portrayals, words in reports, pictures, videos etc of the subjects – visual

We use all of these senses. However, many of us will have a dominant sense and therefore a dominant preference for the way in which we learn. It is actually very easy to elicit the preferred learning style from someone by asking them to describe something, anything, they recently learnt.

So, for instance, adapting the work of Peter R. Scholtes [7], questions may be asked as follows:

Q   What have you learnt recently?
A   Well, I learnt how to change the oil filter on my car
Q   How did you learn that?
A   I learnt it from my neighbour
Q   What did your neighbour do that helped you learn how to do that?

- I *watched* him do it on his car then he *watched* me change the filter on mine – visual preference
- I had him *guide* me through the process of putting the filter on – kinesthetic preference
- He first *explained* what oil filters are for and then he *told* me how to do the job – auditory preference

How many of us are even aware that this information can be gleaned so easily let alone use it? How much more could we learn, and teach, if we targeted the preferred learning styles of the people we manage? How often do we judge others as poor students when we may not have bothered to learn how they learn?

As noted above, the traditional belief system starts from the premise that people need to be controlled and that systems and incentives are based around this premise. Management by objectives, performance appraisal and (often short-term) financial incentives for doing a "good job" are indicative of these systems.

An interesting thought experiment is to consider what the most important issues are to the modern manager. I would suggest that, were you to ask them, not one manager would say "I personally need better goals, objectives and performance standards" or "I personally need better performance appraisal". These tools are based on the idea that "I'm okay, but others in the organisation are not". It is my belief that this is a worrying premise.

The work of both Maslow and Herzberg provide useful models to employ in our efforts to understand each other. Maslow's hierarchy of needs suggests that intrinsic motivation is hierarchical and that we are motivated to satisfy higher needs only when lower levels have been satisfied. The theory is usually shown as a triangle with basic needs of food and shelter at the bottom, rising up through safety and security, social needs and belongingness, followed by self- esteem and then self-fulfilment at the top of the triangle.

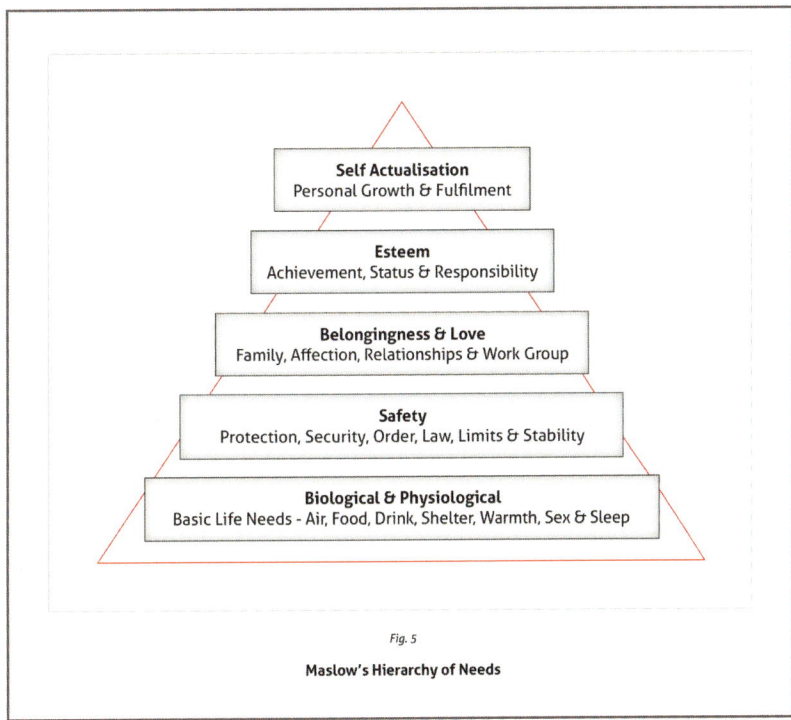

Fig. 5
Maslow's Hierarchy of Needs

However, in the original paper, Maslow stressed that these needs do not rise through the hierarchy in orderly succession. All five needs are always present and their relative importance shifts from lower to higher levels as living standards rise; that is, we all have a variety of needs which we will each seek to meet.

All of the needs will always be present but, as the lower needs are met, it becomes increasingly important to nourish the higher needs. However, if any of the lower needs are threatened, attention returns to the lower need.

Effectively, from a management perspective, we would get more from people if we understood their personal situations and could help them meet any unmet lower level needs so that they could function to their full potential.

Another people thinker, Frederick Herzberg, classified motivation into two categories:

- satisfiers or motivators, which include:
    - achievement, recognition, work itself, responsibility, advancement, personal growth
- dissatisfiers or hygiene factors, which include:
    - organisation policy and administration, supervision, relationship with supervisor, work conditions and salary

Satisfiers, as the name suggests, provide personal motivation and satisfaction. These are the positive feelings that result from intrinsically motivated behaviour. They allow people to satisfy their higher-level needs. Should these factors be absent, people are not dissatisfied, they are simply not satisfied or pleased or particularly motivated.

Conversely, hygiene factors are found to be significant de-motivators when they are lacking. Hygiene factors include the physical work environment and the context in which the work is done. When these basic needs are present, they will not usually increase job satisfaction but, if they are missing, they probably will lead to job dissatisfaction and performance will deteriorate.

The greatest generation of motivation comes from within and is the drive for success and recognition. The more elegantly we can harness our people's talent to the aims and objectives of our organisations, the happier we will be. In order to optimise our organisations, we need to harness the innate intelligence and creativity of our people. These frameworks allow leaders that are interested to create for their people both joy in work and joy in learning.

In short *"The people work IN a system. The manager should work ON the system, to improve it with their help"* [8]. Therefore, a manager's role is as much creative as administrative. Managers need to stimulate those in an organisation to contribute ideas. The job of managers needs to change so that their focus is helping their staff solve problems that are beyond the control of their staff.

Drawing by Alfie Thain, age 7

Part Four
Understanding variation

Like the young doctor in the 1870s, it is with some trepidation that I am suggesting that most managers need to understand variation and understanding variation is a world apart from understanding variance. Effective control of variation is the management equivalent of sterilisation.

The tool to both sterilise and enlighten the organisation is the statistical process control (SPC) chart, which we prefer to call the process *prediction* chart™. Traditionally, its use was to monitor the performance of a process but we can also use it to predict future performance! Yes, not only the future performance and behaviour of your organisation but the knock-on effects within it! The process prediction chart™ is a key part of the armoury needed to deliver real and quantifiable continual improvement.

So, like the young doctor, I need to introduce new thinking; today's managers need to understand that there are two types of variation and these may be due to "special" or "common" causes. And, if you do not understand the differences between these two types of variation, you absolutely cannot be managing a robust performance management system of any kind.

Let me explain….

The performance of all individuals, teams, departments and functions, in fact, the performance of all processes and systems, will vary over time. All activities that can be measured are subject to variation, even if the variation exists only in the way in which the measurements are taken:

- An athlete running the marathon will not run the race in the same time, every time. There will be variation
- A car being built on the assembly line will be assembled from numerous components, many made from a variety of different materials and from a range of suppliers. All of these components, and the car itself, will be subject to variation
- The service provided at a restaurant will also be subject to variation. Different chefs do things differently, the raw material (the food itself) will vary in texture, colour and taste, and the level of service will vary with the training and experience of the waiter assigned to you
- The performance of a telesales operator will vary over time depending on a whole range of issues: the performance of the hardware and software employed, the target market they have been given, the quality of the data provided, the training they have been given, the mood in the centre, the support of the boss, and a vast range of other issues

Numbers in a process go up and down and, every now and then, we get a number that is the highest or lowest for some time. The question is, are these particular numbers any more important than any of the others?

No matter what your process, no matter what your data, all processes and all data display variation. Any measure you can think of will vary from one point in time to another. The trick is to establish the extent of the variation and then to work on the *process* to reduce it but, before we do, we also need to consider cause and effect.

Cause and effect

Most of us assume that the relationship between cause and effect is both simple and direct as in the diagram below:

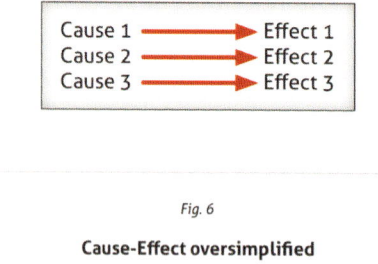

Fig. 6

Cause-Effect oversimplified

In order to properly understand our management systems this model is far too simplistic: day to day reality is far more complex.

Management by objectives suffers from this over simplification. As most of us would expect (and even desire), objectives set in marketing have an effect in sales and operations, objectives set in sales have an effect in operations and service departments and so on. However, when managing staff by objectives, we tend to try and constrain the objectives set for staff in our particular domain and ignore the knock-on implications elsewhere.

Another problem is that the impact of objectives on other people and departments may be small at first and accumulate later. So, in day-to-day reality, the time frames of objectives also need to be considered.

This leads to a more realistic picture of the relationship between cause and effect as shown in Fig. 7 which has been adapted from Dr Michael Tveite's "Ways to think about the World".

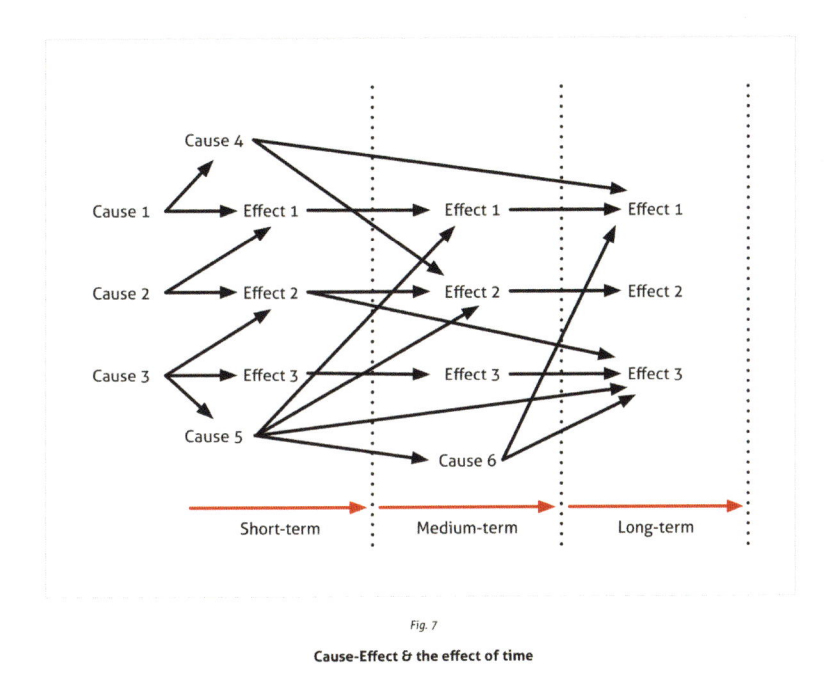

Fig. 7
Cause-Effect & the effect of time

This oversimplification of cause and effect is critical because it has a significant effect on how we perceive variation.

Possible causes of variation are often represented on a cause-effect diagram, which might typically include the branches as shown on Figure 8.

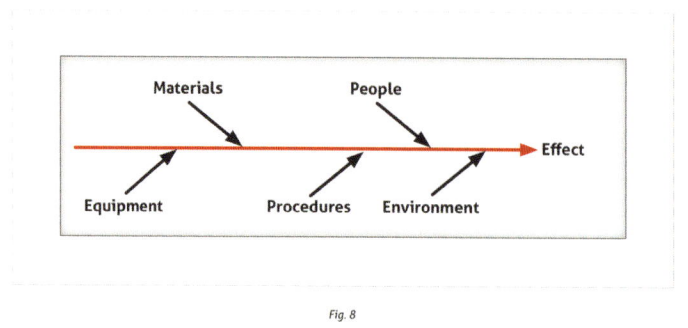

Fig. 8
The Cause-Effect or Fishbone Diagram

Taking the above example of variation in performance of call centre telesales operators, a more complete example of a cause effect diagram has been re-produced in Fig 9. In order to generate this diagram, the sources of variation were brainstormed and the following five arms for the cause-effect diagram were created:

- External factors
- System and support
- Individual factors
- Marketing factors
- Recruitment and training

Further work was then undertaken on each of these to establish lower level causes that might affect the performance of individual operatives.

There are over sixty items on the diagram and only nine over which the individual has any control. One of these is planning and preparation which, it could be argued, has more to do with the training provided by the organisation. We can now see that the system (the environment within which the work is undertaken and the way in which work is designed and managed) has a far bigger influence over variation than the individual.

It is, therefore, not unrealistic to assume that your processes will be subject to dozens, or even hundreds, of cause-effect relationships. However, our culture and, particularly, our management training have led us to the belief that, when confronted with a problem, we need to blame someone - some of us even blame ourselves. But, as we can now clearly see, invariably it is the system that is more likely to be the problem. Dr Joseph Juran suggested that 85% of the time the problem will be in the system and only 15% of the time will it be the worker. Deming, perhaps in a bid to outdo Juran, wrote in The New Economics: "In my experience, most troubles and most possibilities for improvement add up to proportions something like this: 94% belong to the system (the responsibility of management) and 6% are attributable to special causes". Additionally, as was so elegantly stated by the Hopper brothers in their excellent book The Puritan Gift: Reclaiming the American Dream amidst Global Financial Chaos, "In any well run organisation, an individual's achievements were likely to be due as much to the wisdom with which he was directed from above, and to the support of his equals and subordinates, as to his own efforts.". [9]

Fig. 9

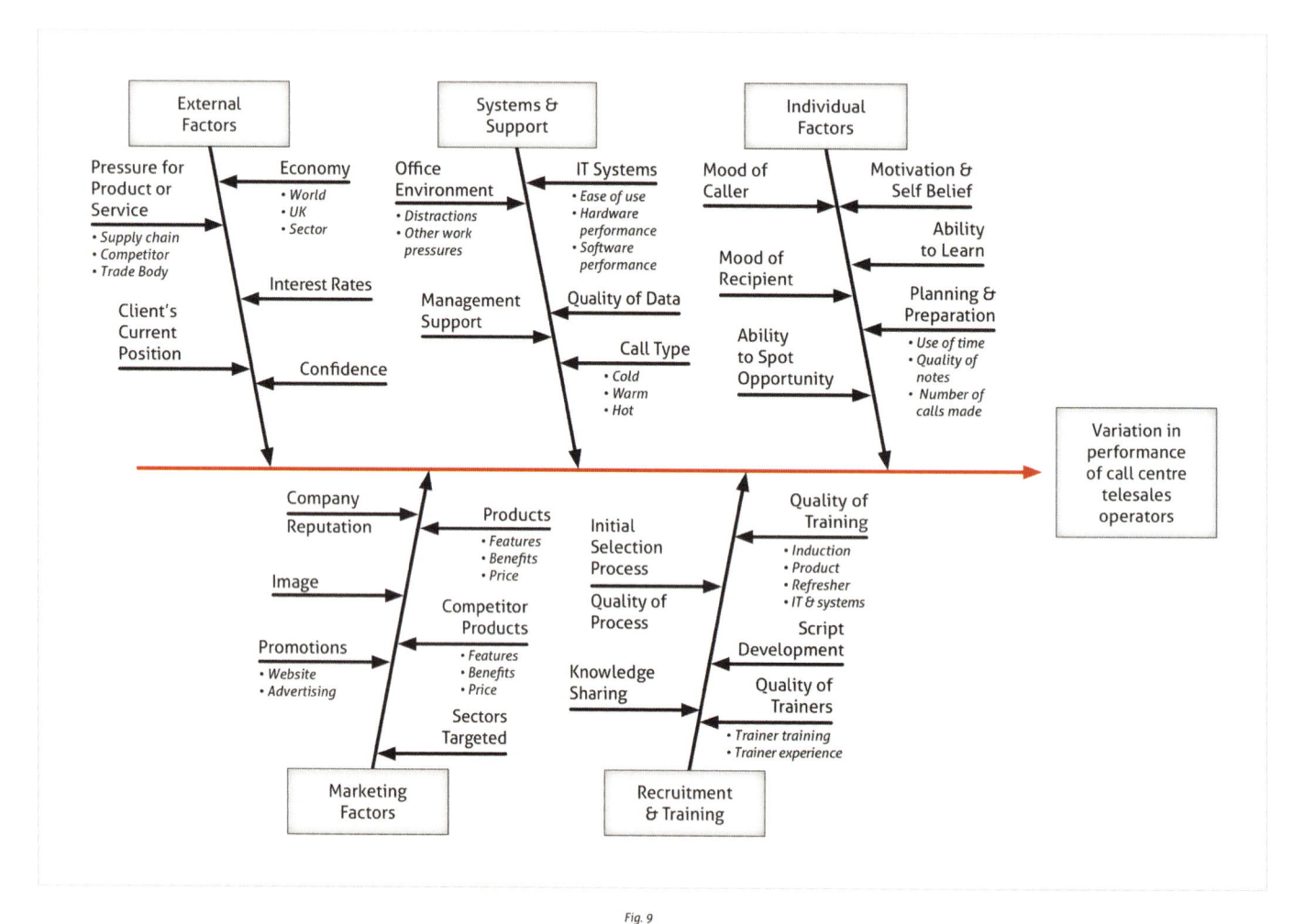

A Cause-Effect diagram showing the potential causes of performance variation in a call centre

Two types of variation

Now we have a more detailed appreciation of cause and effect, we can return to variation.

Whilst every process displays variation, some processes display predictable (common cause) variation while others display unpredictable (special cause) variation. The statistical process control or process prediction chart™, a diagram of which is shown in Figure 10, allows you to see the difference and to take appropriate action for each.

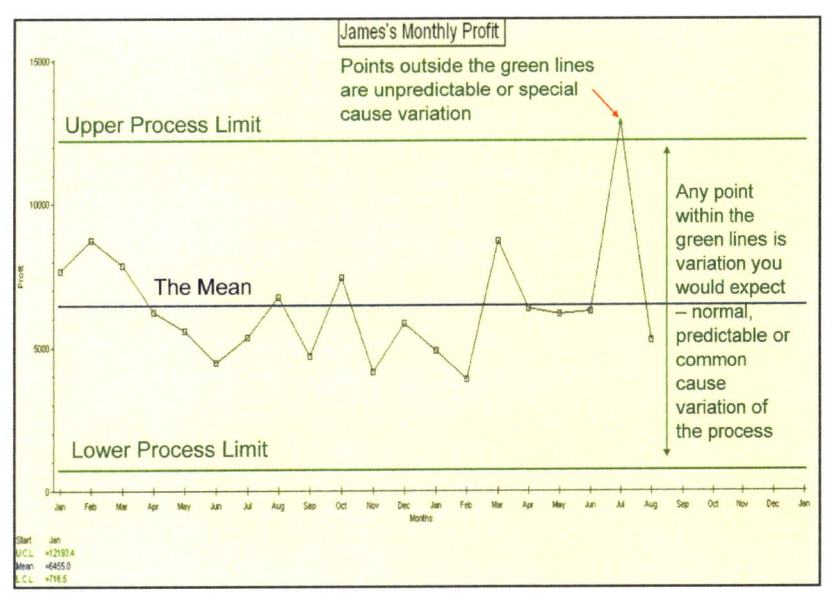

Fig. 10
A process prediction chart™

As the name suggests, common cause variation is the product of a stable process. It is within the bounds of expectation and lies between the upper and lower process limits which can be very easily calculated from the data. On the other hand, special cause variation is outside these limits and beyond the bounds of expectation. Any special causes are worth investigating further in order to eliminate them from the process.

In Figure 10, all of the common cause results, the natural variation of the system, can be seen within the green upper and lower process limits. This means, that if nothing changes, James will be expected to deliver monthly profits of between about £700 and just over £12k. Anything between those figures is just noise.

As another example, you might expect your drive to work to take 30 minutes on average but some days it might take 22 minutes and, equally, some days it might take 38 minutes. This is the range of expectation; the range of natural variation. All processes have this range and all results within this range are effectively equal to one another - a fact which highlights the common misconception that two numbers that are not the same are different - true in mathematics but not true of a process. Also, unlike a journey to work where at some point you will reach a physical minimum journey time, you can work on most management, operations, production and service processes to reduce the expected range and its variation.

Another insight is that there are, in fact, two types of mistakes made when analysing and responding to data:

- Treating a fault, problem, error or complaint as if it was from a special cause when it was actually a common cause; for instance, castigating James for last February's "lousy" profit or patting him on the back for the good March results
- Treating a fault, problem, error or complaint as if it came from a common cause when it was, in fact, due to a special cause; for instance, not investigating James's July result

Not understanding the difference will carry a significant danger of making things worse.

However, in many organisations, monthly reports can be found comparing a whole range of measures critical to the organisation against targets, the same measures for the previous month and, for the very sophisticated, the same measures for the previous year. These measures are then commented upon as either "good" or "bad" depending on how this month's measure compares. This type of "analysis" makes the assumption that measures to which they are being compared are "normal".

Time and time again we read in the papers or see on the TV people who should know better when comparing two points of data. For example: "car sales are up by X% on this time last year", "house prices are down Y% compared to this time last month", "a record number of complaints were made". In his book, The Black Swan [9] Nassim Taleb calls this the Narrative Fallacy and, to slightly paraphrase, suggests "it is as if we want to be wrong with infinite precision (instead of accepting being approximately right)". Presenting data in this way is meaningless. We need to understand the range of variation in the process and then work to reduce it.

There is a better way.

Targets, specifications, the voice of the customer and the voice of the process

Plans, goals, budgets, and targets are all what might be called "specifications". They are what somebody, possibly even ourselves, wants us to achieve. But rarely is any reference made to the current "capability" of the process. Rarely, too, is there any training on how to get from the "as is" situation to the required "to be" situation. This is sad as there are a number of powerful tools that can help us.

As a result of the traditional approach, those lucky enough to show favourable figures get a pat on the back and the unlucky ones with unfavourable figures get kicked a little lower down. Those with favourable figures are "doing okay" while the others are "in trouble". All the while, as is the case most often, the figures are actually within the bounds of expectation. Again, sadly, the assumption is often made that the individual is totally responsible for his performance when, as we have seen, the cause and effect diagram shows there are numerous influences on the performance and many of these have a far more significant effect than the individual.

Again contentious, but, if targets are arbitrary or imposed, managing performance becomes even more fraught with danger. If this month's sales are already above the target, the salesperson may be tempted to "sandbag" excess orders putting them out of the way so they can be used against next month's target. If this month's value is low, then they may be tempted to pull forward marginal or incomplete orders in order to make up the difference.

As Brian Joiner has suggested, when people are pressured to meet a target value, there are three ways they can proceed:

1. They can work to improve the system
2. They can distort the system
3. They can distort the data

Just like the fiasco that ensued when the Government declared that a target should be set for all patients to see their GPs with 24 hours; the doctors got creative and provided us with a system that provided us with exactly that…. but you could only book an appointment that day. Too bad if you were happy to wait a week. Equally, too bad if it was an emergency and all the appointments had already been taken. Another example is the target of reduced waiting lists. The temptation was to bring forward the easy operations. Madness! As Balestracci suggests "…never underestimate how clever frightened human beings can be when faced with a goal". [11]

Before any system can be improved, you need to listen to the Voice of the Process and the Voice of the Process is found on the process prediction chart™.

Sterilising the system, reducing the virus of variation and increasing the degree of predictability requires a study of special and common causes. This is the work of management.

As managers should be the only people changing the system, they are directly responsible for the health of their processes. Without such changes, organisations, like people, get sick.

Obvious questions at this stage include: Do you study and understand variation in your organisation? If not, why not? Also, if you feel you can delegate this responsibility, the question I would ask is "why do we need you"?

Uncontrolled variation leads to chaos, waste and a loss of profit. Reducing the difference between the higher and lower limits is a never ending battle against the virus of variation – the message left for management by Dr Deming.

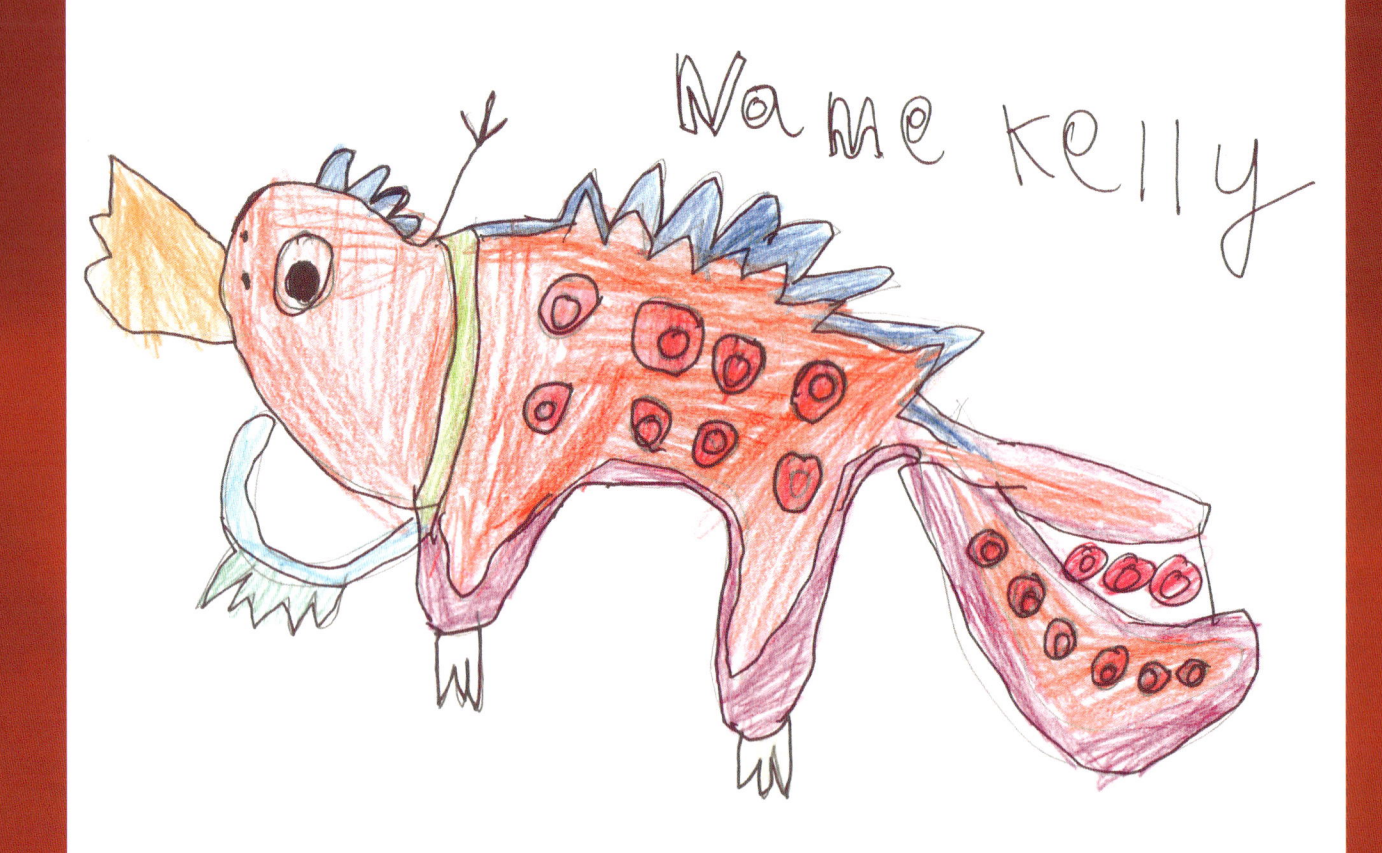

Drawing by Miss Barley Sumpter, age 7

Part Five
Understanding learning

Why is learning so critical for individuals and organisations?

Years ago, knowledge varied little from generation to generation. Now, what the average students learn at school may be out of date by the time they reach their mid 20s. Lifelong learning is no longer a luxury for the individual or for the organisation – it is necessary for survival.

Additionally, the elusive goal of continual improvement cannot be delivered without continual learning and, fortunately for us, there is a structure for acquiring this learning.

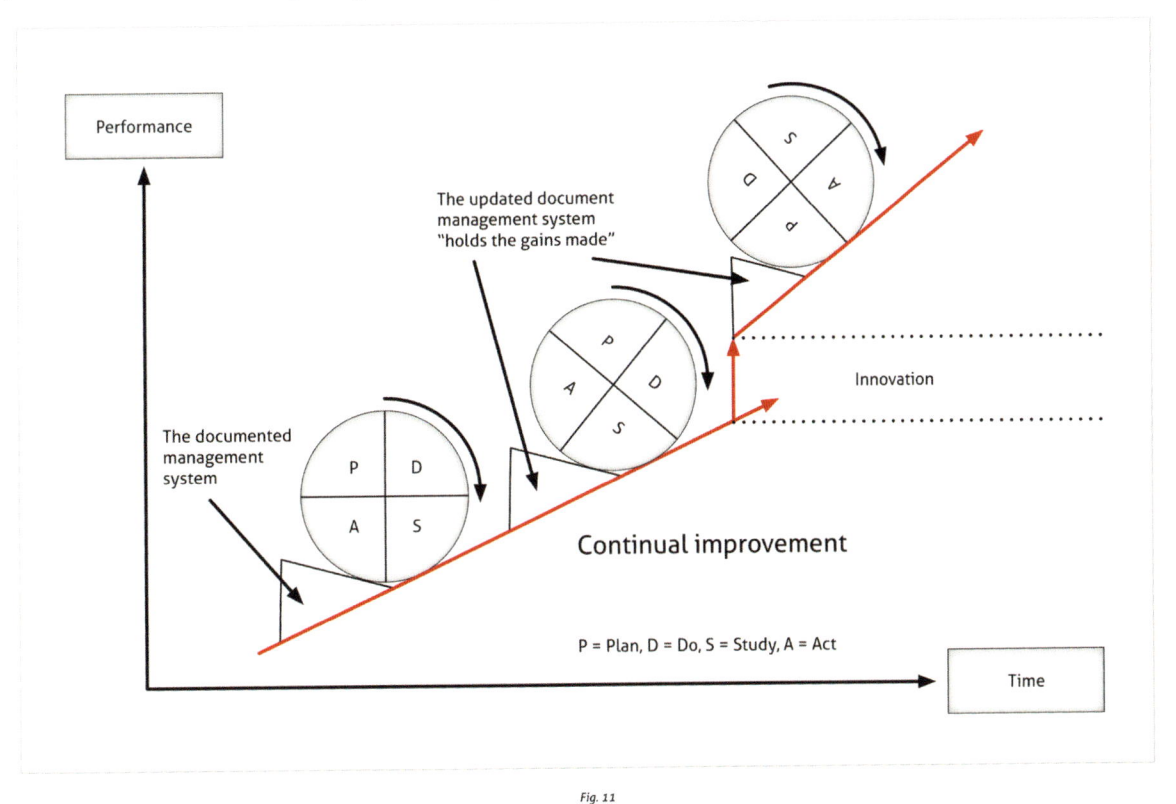

Fig. 11

The Plan, Do, Study, Act Model for learning

The diagram above shows the Plan, Do, Study, Act (PDSA) model for learning which provides the foundation for the systematic and continual improvement of processes. It is an improvement process that involves a cycle of activities. After Act, it begins anew: Plan again, Do again, Study again, Act again - an unending cycle of learning, evaluating, and working on process improvement and capturing benefits.

In more detail, the PDSA cycle comprises:

Plan

The process is first studied to obtain a detailed understanding of the current 'As Is' situation. Then, based on an understanding of the organisation's purpose, its customers' requirements and current and past data, process measures and an improvement plan are formulated.

Do

The changes are made as detailed in the improvement plan. A pilot programme on a small scale is recommended as a first step, if possible. (Large, unstudied changes can lead to large consequences - good and bad!)

Study

The results obtained are compared with the desired results in order to learn from them; the significant difference between a "change" and an "improvement" being seen easily on a process prediction chart™.

Act

Take advantage of what you have learned. Decide what you will try next. The question at this point is: Do you continue to improve? If so, go around the cycle again. If not, standardise the new process, for instance, by locking the gain into any documented operating procedures. Then plan again, but for a different improvement project.

This process can be seen from Figure 11. Sitting behind the PDSA wheel is a wedge, essentially the organisation's documented management system; the organisation's standing orders, operating instructions or perhaps an ISO registered system. Regardless, training needs to be provided and the documented management system must be updated to hold the gains made.

The PDSA model is a driver of both organisational learning and, of all things, forgiveness. Essentially, the underlying premise is "let's do the very best we can" but then commit to studying what we did so that we may learn and improve. The PDSA model values curiosity. It provides us with a structure and the structure allows us to make mistakes, as long as we learn from them. The PDSA model provides a framework for lifelong learning.

Measurement - From chaos to order and prediction

Using the PDSA method, the chart in Figure 12 shows how a team learnt to understand the cycle time for an order processing department. Initially, data collected shows that the process is in chaos with the time taken to process each order increasing as each order is received (orders 11-25). Having studied the data, the team pooled its ideas and drew up an improvement plan. A number of changes were then made.

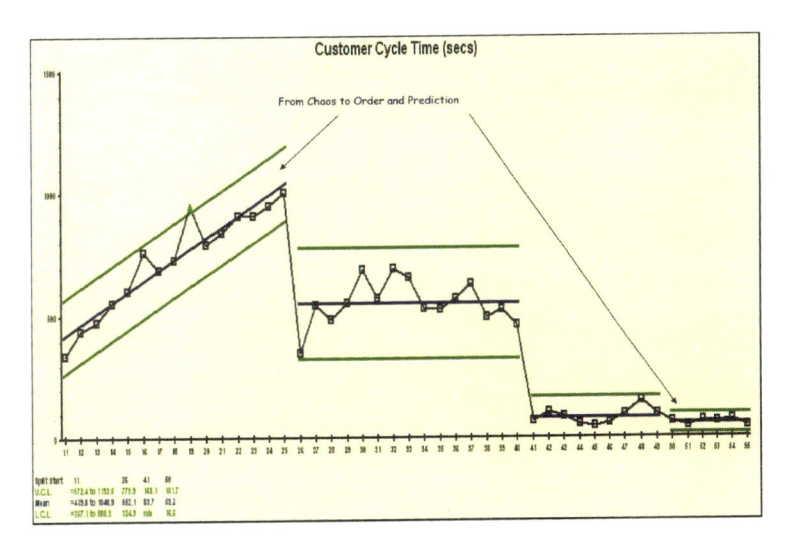

Fig. 12
From chaos to order and prediction

The second section on the graph (orders 26-40) shows the first improvement after these changes. The chart shows that the process is now far more stable but, by repeating the improvement cycle (orders 41-49 and 50-55), the process is, without any capital investment, significantly improved yet again. The result of the second and third improvement plan is that orders can now be processed considerably faster than had ever been imagined. The impact is significant. The capacity has been massively increased. The time taken to process an order initially varied between about 400 and 1000 seconds. At the end of the continual improvement process, the time taken to process an order was less than 60 seconds. The implications are profound: approximately 10 times as much work can be achieved with the same staff levels, staff can be re-deployed to more value-adding jobs, a completely new level of service can be provided, and waste has been removed from the process.

Obviously, however, order processing time may not be a key metric for your organisation. It is therefore possible, and indeed highly desirable, to use the systems diagram to establish the key measures for each process (there may be more than one key measure for each process) and then to arrange graphs, like the one above, on a Performance Dashboard® as detailed in Figure 13. This Performance Dashboard® shows a composite of results for a construction company and it is not difficult to see how the chief executive might have a dashboard showing perhaps new business, sales, profit, cash in the bank, productivity, customer retention, customer satisfaction and any other measure of interest, whilst the finance director will have another (different) Performance Dashboard®, the construction director another and the site managers another again.

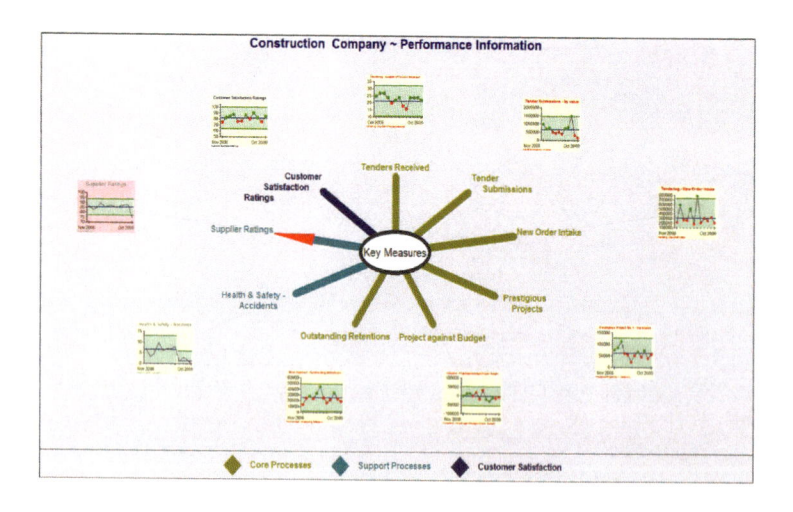

Fig. 13
The Performance Dashboard®

Essentially, what we need to create, in order to align the measurement system to the management system, to the processes and to the organisation's purpose, is a connected set of measures that work both up and down and through the organisation. This can be seen from Figure 14. The key point is that the measurement system needs to be geared to how each layer of management adds value to the organisation.

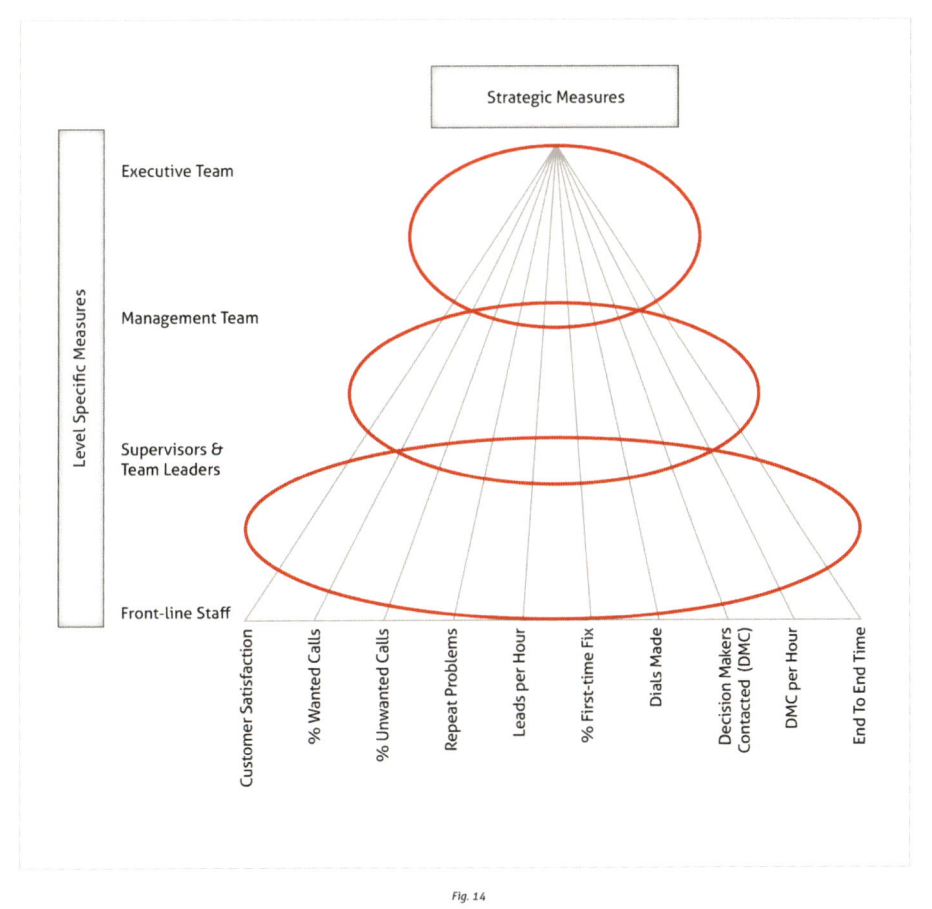

Fig. 14
**Differing levels of management need to look at
differing perspectives, and add value differently**

However, whilst measurement can show that important improvements have been delivered, there is a caveat - some of the most important numbers are both unknown and unknowable. Business schools have taught managers to think solely quantitatively, not quantitatively *and* qualitatively, as managers of systems, people, learning and knowledge. How do you put a value on knowledge, learning, experience, morale, honesty, integrity or devotion? Management is a craft; as much an art as it is a science.

Drago!

Land of the dragon's

Drawing by Miss Madison Lockwood

Part Six
Dragon slaying

Optimising the whole of an organisation involves examining an elaborate mix of people, performance and systems, and then building on the knowledge gained. The traditional approach of examining each of these components individually leads us to the question "Why do our efforts to improve things go wrong so often"? The simple answer is that this integrated approach is not usually taught in business schools and managers do not currently recognise the interrelatedness of the components in the above model. As well as their technical and operational specialisms, managers need to manage people and processes. Critically, however, managers also need to manage points at which their processes interact with other processes in order to deliver on the organisation's purpose and deliver value to the customer. This is rarely effectively executed. Any attempt to isolate and analyse individual components of an organisation is as ineffective as the sprinter, Usain Bolt, analysing his feet when he is tired from running.

So let's slay a few dragons. Starting with our management model introduced in figures 1-3:

- **Purpose**
  The purpose is different to what the organisation does. Blockbuster Video rented videos; but their purpose could probably be articulated as something like "providing entertainment and education for people in their own homes, at a time of their choosing". Carburettor manufacturers produced carburettors; their purpose could have been something like "getting an efficient fuel/air mix into an internal combustion engine". Blockbuster Video and most of the carburettor manufacturers are no longer with us! They focused on what they did, not the benefits and capabilities they should have been delivering - their purpose
- **Systems**
  The current reality is usually far more complex than is realised, not least because cause and effect are separated in both time and often departmental and divisional space
- **People**
  All systems are driven by, and include, people who have free will and often resist being "told" to change. It is also rare for people to be engaged with the greater good of what an organisation is trying to achieve
- **Variation**
  Most organisations focus on variance; variation is rarely acknowledged and variation is present in all management and operational processes
- **Knowledge**
  Effective change is about predicting the future so plans need to be based on sound theories; the "suck it and see" approach will only work if you get lucky! Each time an organisation submits a quotation or tender they are predicting they will make some money. Rarely is the prediction tested in order to learn and improve.

Management myths

At the start of this book, the next bullet points would have been very contentious. Hopefully, now, with some ideas about a holistic model of management, they are less so:

- Robust performance measurement cannot be managed effectively without understanding variation. There are two type of variation: common cause and special cause and, without understanding the difference, managers make the mistake of confusing the two which has a high probability of making things worse!
- Robust people management cannot occur if variation in people is not accounted for. There is variation in people but we would suggest there is significantly more variation in the "system". Tools such as management by objectives and performance appraisals, make the assumption that the performance of an individual is a result of only their efforts and is not influenced by the system in which they work. This is just not true.
- Robust performance improvement cannot occur if the organisation is only being managed as a hierarchy, as the tendency is to optimise the individual functions or departments which will usually sub optimise the system as a whole. The organisation needs to be managed as a system.
- Robust performance improvement cannot take place unless the organisation learns and, in order to learn, it must fully appreciate the complexity associated with cause and effect.
- Robust performance management cannot occur if people are incentivised by *individual* financial gain. Win-win situations need to be engineered so that everyone in the system benefits. Real trust needs to be developed and the intrinsic motivation created by doing a good and worthwhile job needs to be nurtured.

Drawing by Mr George "Monkey Dog" Woods, age 7

Part Seven
Conclusion

In applying these principles, arguably irrefutable laws, of management, it is entirely possible to deliver real and lasting improvement. In order to do so, it is first necessary to understand the system that is being worked within, to excite people to the aim of the system, and to create a learning environment where we can constantly improve the way in which work works so that we can be sure we meet, or even exceed, our customers' expectations.

Again, an extract from The Puritan Gift, a Financial Times top 10 business book of the year:

> *"The paradox is that by <u>not</u> pursuing profit to the exclusion of all else, the Great Engine companies (of America) would achieve enormous increases in the value of their net assets, whereas, by single-mindedly pursuing profit on behalf of their new masters after 1970, these same companies and their successors actually created less genuine lasting wealth, indeed, they would destroy it".*[12]

This book has been about challenging thinking. Should you subscribe to our view, I can promise the change will not be easy nor will it be quick. What it will be is hard work, fun, liberating and, to many, there may well be a sense of relief.

However, just as changing the mind-set of the distinguished physicians would not have been sufficient in itself to guarantee change, neither is changing your mind. The mind-set of the organisation needs to change. The approach to problems needs to change. The approach to data needs to change. The approach to customers needs to change. Strategies need to change. Practices and procedures need to change. Training, coaching and education programmes need to be put in place.[13] With the distinguished physicians, patients died. In your organisation, key people may well leave: they may not adapt to the change. My last question is: "can you"?

There is a better way to manage and I hope my thoughts have whetted your appetite. To discuss the issues raised or, as Keith suggested in the foreword, to become part of the story, please feel free to contact me on 0044 7976 426 286 or mwoods@statius.uk.com

References

The books and references are many and varied and include authors like Julian Russell, Henry Neave, Brian Joiner, Don Wheeler, Denis Sherwood, Joseph O'Conner and Robert Dilts, to name just a select few.

Specific references include:

[1] TRIBUS, Myron, *The Germ Theory of Management.* Deming Forum W2 (Revised 2007), page 9.

[2] DEMING, W. Edwards, *Out of the Crisis*. Massachusetts Institute of Technology (1982), pages 465-466.

[3] SCHOLTES, Peter R, *The Leader's Handbook.* McGraw Hill (1998), page 2.

[4] SEDDON, John, *Back to the Method.* Quality World, Sept 2009

[5] PELLEY, Jay, LinkedIn, The W. Edwards Deming Institute Official Group 15th December 2010

[6] Personal correspondence with Stuart Swalwell regarding the thoughts of Art Kleiner

[7] SCHOLTES, Peter R, *Learning and Leadership.* Deming Forum W4 (1994)

[8] TRIBUS, Myron, *The Germ Theory of Management.* Deming Forum W2 (Revised 2007), page 26.

[9] HOPPER, Kenneth and William, *The Puritan Gift: Reclaiming the American Dream amidst Global Financial Chaos.* I B Tauris (2007) page 135.

[10] TALEB, Nassim Nicholas, *The Black Swan; The impact of the highly improbable..* Penguin Books (2007).

[11] BALESTRACCI, Davis, *Statistical Thinking Applied to Everyday Data*

[12] HOPPER, Kenneth and William, *The Puritan Gift: Reclaiming the American Dream amidst Global Financial Chaos.* I B Tauris (2007), page 225.

[13] RAJAH, Kanes K & DeCOURSEY, Adie, Neuro Linguistic Programming: NLP for Executive and Professional Development, University of Greenwich Press (2009).

INDEX

A

aim, 5, 9, 12-13, 18, 43
appraisal, 16, 40
auditory, 15-16

B

benefits, 1, 34, 39-40

C

capabilities, 12, 29, 39
cause-effect, 23-24
change management, viii, x-xi, 43
chaos, 30, 35
common cause variation, 27
competition, 6
continual improvement, 4, 21, 33-35
core processes, 10
cost(s), 10, 12
customer, 9-10
customer needs, 9-10

D

data, 27-29
Deming, Edwards, x-xiii, 3, 6, 25, 30
de-motivators, 18
dissatisfaction, 18
dissatisfiers, 18

dominant sense, 15-16

E

expectation, 27-28

F

family tree, 9
feedback, xiii, 10

G

goals, viii, 12, 16, 29

H

Herzberg, Frederick, 18
hierarchy of needs, 16-17
Hopper, Kenneth, 25
Hopper, William, 25
hygiene factors, 18

I

improved performance, 1
incentives, 16
input, 10
intrinsic motivation, 16, 40
ISO (International Standards Organization), 10, 34

K

kinaesthetic, 15

L

Leadership, 12, 18
learn, 1, 3-4, 9, 13, 15-16
learning
   lifelong, 33-34
listening
   to customers and stakeholders, 1
lower process limit, 27

M

management by objectives, 16, 22, 40
Maslow, Abraham, 16-17
measurement, 35-37, 40
measurement systems, 9-10, 36
mission, 13
motivate, 13, 16, 18
motivation, 15-16, 18, 40

N

natural variation, 27-28

O

objectives, 12, 18
   management by, 16, 22, 40
optimised, 9
optimum performance, 4
organisational chart, 9-10
organisational purpose, 12
output, 10

P

PDSA (Plan, Do, Study, Act), 34-35
people, 4, 6, 12-13, 15-18
performance
   improved, 1
Performance Dashboard™, xiii, 12, 36
performance standards, 16
predictable variation, 27
preferred learning style, 16
procedures, 9-10, 12, 15, 34, 43
process
   behaviour chart, viii, 6, 18, 21
   capability, 29
   limits, 27, 30
      lower, 30
      upper, 27
   measures, 28, 34, 36
   voice of the, 29
processes, 12-13, 27-30, 34-36, 39
   sub, 10
profit, 10, 12
purpose
   organisational, 12

S

satisfaction, 18, 36
satisfiers, 18
Scholtes, Peter R., 16
Seddon, John, x, 9
sense, 6, 15-16, 43

short-term thinking, 6
SPC (statistical process control), 21, 27
special cause variation, 27
specifications, 29
sub optimised, 9
subprocesses, 10
suppliers, xi, 9, 21
systems, 16, 21-22
systems diagram, 9-10, 12, 36
systems thinking, viii, x-xi, 3

T

target, 9, 12, 16, 21, 28-29
targets, 12, 28-29
trust, xiii, 40

U

understanding learning, 33
understanding people, 4, 15
understanding the organisation as a system, 9
understanding variation, 4, 21, 40
unpredictable variation, 27
upper process limit, 27

V

value adding processes, 10
variation, 4, 21-24, 30, 39-40
   common cause, predictable, 27-28, 30, 40
   natural, 27-28
   special cause, unpredictable, 25, 27-28, 40
vision, xiii, 9, 12-13, 18, 39
visual, 15

W

waste(s), 10, 30, 35
Whistler, Major, 9
work, x-xiii, 3-4, 9-10, 12-13, 15-16, 35-36